...by night

Remarkable Years

GUINNESS®

AN OFFICIAL CELEBRATION OF 250 REMARKABLE YEARS

HISTORY ▽ ADVERTS ▽ RECIPES

hamlyn

An Hachette UK Company
www.hachette.co.uk

First published in Great Britain in 2009 by
Hamlyn, a division of Octopus Publishing Group Ltd
2–4 Heron Quays, London E14 4JP
www.octopusbooks.co.uk

Text and design copyright © Octopus Publishing Group Limited 2009
Recipe text copyright © Paul Hartley 2009

Paul Hartley asserts his moral right to be identified as the author
of the recipes in this book.

The GUINNESS word and HARP device are trademarks of
Guinness & Co. and are used under licence by Octopus Publishing
Group Limited.

ISBN 978-0-600-61988-8

A CIP catalogue record for this book is available from the British Library.

Printed and bound in China   0

10 9 8 7 6 5 4 3 2 1

Contents

Introduction: 250 years of Guinness

In the beginning of the story of my family there was Arthur. He was a brewer and a family man but he was also a radical visionary.

At a time when there were so many failing breweries in Dublin, very few can have thought that Arthur's purchase of the lease on St James's Gate would be a good idea. But Arthur must have had incredible self-belief and determination to make his dream of having a brewery in Dublin become a reality.

The location that he chose was exceptional. The St James's Gate Brewery had all the benefits of wonderful fresh water sourced from the Rivers Dodder and Poddle, yet the waterways also provided him with the ability to import the finest of ingredients from the countryside. His customers were very close. Only a visionary like Arthur would have spotted the potential of a site which had lain derelict for so many years.

And so Arthur was to begin a family history of brewing which was to last for five generations. Each generation persisted with Arthur's vision of quality. This in turn meant that the company was at the forefront of science, of transportation and of marketing.

If there is an ethos that overrides Arthur's entrepreneurial skills, it is that Guinness should be enjoyed – enjoyed with friends and enjoyed with delicious food. So Arthur would be extremely proud (and probably amazed) to be involved with this wonderful, and scrumptious, book.

Rory Guinness
Son of last Guinness family chairman Benjamin Iveagh, and Guinness author

RIGHT *Loading casks of Guinness beer on to the Liffey barge* Clonsilla. *The SS* Carrowdore, *also owned by the Guinness Company, is berthed alongside the Custom House in the background.*

THE STORY OF GUINNESS

Arthur Guinness

The man who began it all, Arthur Guinness was born in 1725 in Celbridge, County Kildare. His father, Richard, was land steward to the Reverend Arthur Price, who later became the Archbishop of Cashel. Arthur Guinness was named in honour of the Archbishop, who was his godfather.

1759	Brewery founded by Arthur Guinness
1803	Arthur Guinness II inherits the brewery
1855	Brewery passed on to Benjamin Lee Guinness
1868	Benjamin's sons Arthur Edward and Edward Cecil inherit the brewery
1876	Edward Cecil buys out Arthur Edward and becomes sole proprietor
1886	Brewery incorporated on London Stock Exchange

ABOVE *Arthur Guinness (1725–1803) began with a small brewery and went on to be one of Ireland's most successful brewers and the founder of a worldwide brewing phenomenon.*

RIGHT *The stamp depicting Arthur Guinness that was issued in 1959 to mark the bicentenary of the founding of the Guinness Brewery.*

Brewing in the blood

Richard's duties as land steward included brewing ale for the workers on the Archbishop's estate and Arthur Guinness learned the fundamentals of brewing from his father as he was growing up. In 1752 the Archbishop died, leaving Arthur and his father a generous legacy of £100 each. Arthur used the money to open a small brewery in Leixlip, a village on the upper reaches of the River Liffey, about 17 km (10½ miles) from Dublin. A few years later, at the age of 34, Arthur left this brewery to be managed by his younger brother Richard and set off for Dublin.

Here, on 31 December 1759, he signed a lease on a brewery on James's Street. The brewery was dilapidated and badly equipped. Add to this the fact that there were already more than 60 breweries in Dublin providing stiff competition, and there must surely have been those who questioned Arthur's judgement. But his passion and perseverance were to prove all doubters wrong.

In 1761 Arthur Guinness married Dublin heiress Olivia Whitmore, and they went on to have 21 children. Ten of these children survived to establish a dynasty that would spread to many countries. By 1767 Arthur Guinness was Master of the Dublin Corporation of Brewers.

Like all brewers, Arthur was dependent on a good supply of water and, as part of his lease, he was entitled to free water. When, in 1775, he was accused by the Corporation of Dublin of breaching the watercourse to take more water than he was entitled to, Arthur vowed to defend his water supply. When the city's sheriff arrived at the brewery with a team of men intent on cutting off its water supply,

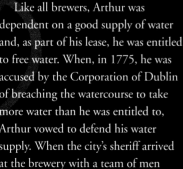

they were met by Arthur and his employees. Arthur grabbed a pickaxe and confronted the sheriff and his men, refusing to let them proceed. He was a man completely committed to his brewery. Although there was no disruption to the water supply, the litigation over this issue between the Corporation of Dublin and Arthur Guinness was to drag on for ten years before it was finally resolved.

When Arthur Guinness died in 1803 at the age of 78, his estate was valued at £23,000 – truly a fortune.

Porter please

Arthur began by making an ale at the brewery, but in 1799 the decision was taken to brew only porter – an inspired move that led to the beer that we know as Guinness today.

The invention of porter is attributed to a man called Ralph Harwood who was brewing beer in Shoreditch, London, in 1722. Porter was so-called because it was the popular choice of the porters who worked at many London markets. It was brewed using roasted barley, which gave it a distinctive dark colour and taste, and improved on keeping in wooden barrels.

'We are brewers and always have been.'
Rupert Guinness, Chairman's speech, 1949

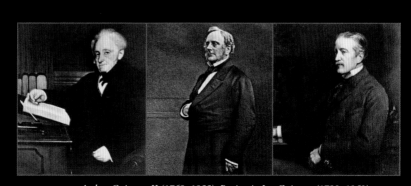

LEFT TO RIGHT *Arthur Guinness II (1768–1855), Benjamin Lee Guinness (1798–1868), Sir Edward Cecil Guinness, 1st Earl of Iveagh (1847–1927).*

St James's Gate

Arthur Guinness must have been very confident that his beer would be a success, as he signed a 9,000-year lease on the brewery at St James's Gate. The rent payable on the site was £45 a year.

By 1798 it was one of the largest employers in Dublin, by 1833 it was the largest brewery in Ireland and by the 1880s it was the largest brewery in the world.

The place

When Arthur acquired the rundown brewery, it had ceased brewing and had been on the market for nearly ten years. It covered an area of 1.62 hectares (4 acres) and much of the brewing equipment was in a bad state of repair. Included on the site were a copper, a kieve (see page 36), two malthouses, stabling for a dozen horses and a loft to hold about 200 tonnes of hay.

Despite these simple beginnings, Arthur quickly built up his trade and developed and expanded the brewery, so that by the end of the 19th century it had grown from 1.62 hectares (4 acres) to 24.3 hectares (60 acres).

Now, in the 21st century, the St James's Gate Brewery covers an area of 26 hectares (64 acres). It is one of the most technologically advanced breweries in the world and produces 8 million kegs of Guinness every year.

Guinness Storehouse at St James's Gate, topped by the Gravity Bar that has 360-degree views over Dublin, is the most visited tourist attraction in Ireland.

ABOVE A showcard from the 1880s containing illustrations of the Brewery.

ABOVE A 19th-century illustration showing an artificially wide gate so the Brewery can be seen.

MAIN PICTURE *A lorry pulls out of the front gate of the Brewery in 1948.*

INSET *The entrance to the St James's Gate Brewery today.*

The tap

Every male employee over the age of 21 was given a free beer allowance of two pints each day, served at 'The Tap'. St James's Gate Brewery had three taps located around the site: Back Gate Tap, Traffic Tap and Container Tap. Men who had physically demanding jobs or who did three hours or more overtime were given an extra pint.

In the early 1970s the taps were closed and employees got their beer in bottles to take home with them. Employees still receive a beer allowance to this day, but they are encouraged to drink it at home!

The people

Described as 'a city within a city', by the end of the 19th century the St James's Gate Brewery employed over 3,000 people and it was estimated that 1 in every 30 people in Dublin was financially dependent on the brewery. The workforce included occupations as diverse as mouse catchers and clockmakers.

The site had its own internal railway, fire brigade, electrical power station, a postal system – a miniature version of the public post office – and its own uniformed police force.

In the 1930s St James's Gate employed about 500 craftsmen, including plumbers, fitters, carpenters and electricians, to maintain machinery and buildings. Working alongside them at the brewery were, among others, brewers, waitresses, clerks, chemists, medical staff, catering staff, stable workers and coopers.

Benefits

Brewery employees in the late 19th century were among the highest paid in Dublin and received employment benefits that were rare for the time, including pensions, housing and medical care.

In 1870 a medical officer was appointed and a dispensary opened. In 1888 the brewery employed a full-time midwife for the wives of brewery workers and cookery classes were organized in the late 1890s to teach brewery wives about good nutrition.

TOP LEFT A group of visitors taste the beer in the visitors' sample room in 1906.

TOP MIDDLE Waitresses at one Brewery restaurant enjoy a well-earned rest and a bottle of Guinness stout in 1957.

TOP RIGHT Clerks at work in the busy St James's Gate cask records office in 1949.

FAR LEFT Some of the Brewery's on-site firemen with their Merryweather fire engine in about 1930.

The cooper's craft

Wooden casks were used by the Guinness Company for transporting and storing beer for almost 200 years. The men who made these casks were the coopers and their trade was an important one at the brewery. By the 1920s about 300 coopers, making 1,000 casks a week, were employed.

Father and son

Being a cooper was a very prestigious job and the only one at the brewery that was paid on a piecework basis. Instead of earning a weekly wage, some of the coopers were paid for each cask they made or repaired, so the best and fast coopers made good money.

It took an apprenticeship of up to seven years to learn all the skills that went into being a cooper and the trade was a closed one, passed from father to son in each family. As an apprentice, a young cooper was not allowed to drink alcohol and needed his master's consent to marry.

Sniffing out trouble

All casks returned to the brewery were smelled to check whether they were 'sweet' or 'foul'. Foul casks were the ones that had been left lying empty too long and these were sent for extra cleansing and steaming.

Specially appointed coopers were given the task of sniffing out foul casks, and they underwent regular checks to make sure that they had not lost their sense of smell. Senior coopers also acted as 'smellers', but they were too important to bend down; instead two apprentices would lift each cask for the senior coopers to smell.

The last cask

In 1946 aluminium kegs were introduced and were used alongside wooden casks for many years, but by 1961 there were only 70 coopers left at the brewery and, in March 1963, the last wooden cask was filled.

The Guinness Company kept on some coopers to make furniture – such as umbrella stands, tables, plant containers and cocktail cabinets – out of the redundant casks, but this stopped altogether as coopers gradually retired and the stocks of casks were used up.

ABOVE *A smeller uses his trained sense of smell to check whether a returned barrel is 'sweet' or 'foul'.*

Casks come in many sizes:

Firkin — holds 36.4 litres (8 gallons/64 pints)

Kilderkin — holds 72.7 litres (16 gallons/128 pints)

Barrel — holds 145.5 litres (32 gallons/256 pints)

Hogshead — holds 236.4 litres (52 gallons/416 pints)

Butt — holds 472.8 litres (104 gallons/832 pints)

ABOVE General view of the cooperage workshop with coopers at work, 1948.

In 1900 there were 320,000 casks, which could hold 41 million pints when full and – stacked as a pyramid – would be as high as the Eiffel Tower

Making a cask

First, the cooper hand selected his timber, almost always American white oak, which was strong enough to withstand the rough handling of the brewery trade.

Then the process of making a cask could begin, and what a process it was, involving over 30 different tools, enormous physical effort and a range of skills from carpentry to blacksmithing. Neither glue nor nails were used in making the casks.

The cooper began by preparing the staves, the individual pieces of wood that form the cask. First he cut each stave roughly to shape with an axe, then used several different knives to hone each stave to the exact, slightly curved shape. The staves were passed over a jointer – a freestanding plane – and their edges angled so that they would join smoothly.

The staves were then gathered and placed upright inside a metal hoop, forming the cask shape. This was known as 'raising up'.

A machine called a steam bell was lowered over the staves. The steam bell used high-pressure steam to soften the wood and make it pliable.

The steam bell was removed and the cooper used a rope to bring the splayed ends together. Temporary hoops were hammered over the staves, forcing them into the characteristic curved cask shape. The inside of the cask was then charred by building a small fire inside to remove the remaining acidity from the wood and to seal the wood. This part of the process was very tricky to judge.

The cooper prepared the cask ends for their lids, which were called 'heads', by cutting a groove for them to fit.

The only time the cooper used a measuring tool was when he used a compass to measure the cask ends. For all the other stages in making a cask he was able to judge for precision by eye alone – a truly astounding skill.

The cooper used specially shaped paring tools to smooth the surfaces and then the heads were slotted securely into the grooves at each end of the cask. Bungholes were made in the side of the cask.

A set of wrought-iron hoops was tailor-made for each cask, to replace the temporary hoops. The hoops were hammered into place over the staves. Finally, the cask was branded with an identification number and the word 'Guinness', and then it was ready to be filled.

Getting the beer there

From the horse-drawn carts of the 19th century to the sleek bulk-liquid carriers of the 21st, modes of transporting Guinness from brewery to drinker have seen many changes over the years.

The dray days

Horses provided the main form of transport in the early days, both to deliver beer and for moving loads around the brewery site. When the Grand Canal opened in the mid-18th century, horses were used to draw the barges loaded with casks along the River Shannon as, for the first time, Guinness became available outside Dublin.

There were stables inside the St James's Gate site for 12 horses initially and by 1891 there were 150 dray horses, including some hired from a local company. The horses were so important to the brewery that a company veterinary surgeon was appointed and the draymen followed detailed guidelines for their care. The guidelines included recipes for each of the three meals that the horses were fed each day. Reputedly, the horses also received a ration of beer in their daily mash!

On a busy day, up to 40 teams of two or three draymen and a horse – each horse carrying a 2-tonne load – would travel around Dublin delivering casks of beer to public houses. For heavier loads, horses were used in twos and they had paired names, including Rhyme and Reason and Thunder and Lightning.

On the first day of every month, all draymen and their horses were fully inspected – the men and their uniforms, the horses and the carts – and the best turned-out received a bonus.

Motorized transport began to take over, and in 1932 the Guinness Company sold their own team of Clydesdales and Pecherons and hired in the few horses that they still employed. The last horse to be used on brewery business was pensioned off in 1960.

ABOVE *Draymen with their horses outside the stable at the Brewery in about 1885.*

TOP LEFT *The scene outside John Kehoe's pub in South Anne Street, Dublin, circa 1955, as one of the last town deliveries is made.*

TOP RIGHT *Lorries laden with casks pull out of the loading bay at the Brewery, 1948.*

RIGHT *Loading barrels on the Grand Canal at the rear of the Guinness Brewery in 1955.*

MAIN PICTURE *Locomotives, carriages and horse-drawn carts move casks from the loading bay on a typically busy day in the early 1900s.*

INSET *The rail tunnel and, alongside it, the pedestrian tunnel that connected the upper and lower levels of St James's Gate, circa 1906.*

Steaming ahead

In 1873 the brewery grew substantially when it acquired land bordering the River Liffey. The brewery was now divided into two, with an upper level and a lower level, separated by James's Street. With the site so spread out, horsepower was no longer enough and an efficient way of moving casks and other material around became essential.

An extensive railway system, covering a total of 13 km (8 miles), was designed by Samuel Geoghegan, chief engineer at the brewery, and construction began in 1875. Two problems had to be overcome. The first was that the track had to be narrow enough to navigate around awkward spaces at the brewery, but it also had to connect with the broad-gauge track used by the Irish rail network outside the brewery. The solution was to lay both types of track: narrow inside the brewery and broad-gauge to connect to the track outside. Special 'haulage wagons' were then designed. The narrow-gauge locomotives were hoisted on to these and the drive from their wheels was transmitted to the wagons' wheels, allowing them to use the broad-gauge tracks.

The second obstacle was the 15.25-metre (50-foot) difference in height between the upper and lower levels of the brewery. A great feat of engineering was devised to overcome this: a spiral tunnel, similar to those designed for tunnels through the Alps, that gradually wound down from the upper to lower levels. This tunnel cost £3,000 to construct, an astounding amount of money for the time.

The Guinness Company started out with five coal-fired steam locomotives, including two 5-tonne engines nicknamed 'Hops' and 'Malt'. These engines weren't entirely suitable for the narrow-gauge track and so Samuel Geoghegan, a very resourceful engineer, designed his own locomotive engines for use at the brewery. The fleet of locomotives grew to more than 20 and the railway – the tracks of which can still be seen at St James's Gate today – was used right up until 1975.

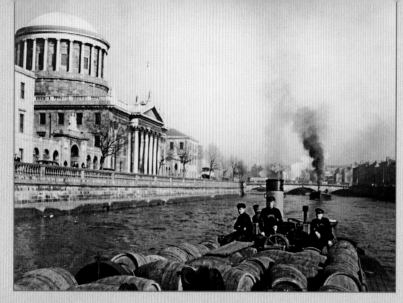

MAIN PICTURE *Barges alongside the jetty at the north end of St James's Gate are loaded with wooden casks in 1910.*

INSET *A Guinness Company barge makes its way along the River Liffey in about 1950.*

24

The Liffey barges

In 1873 Guinness built their own jetty on the River Liffey and the first river barges, which were to become a familiar and much-loved Dublin sight, were commissioned. These early barges were steam-operated and all named after rivers around Ireland.

In 1927 a new type of barge was introduced. This fleet of barges, each named after places around Dublin, could do the 1.6-km (1-mile) journey from the brewery jetty to Dublin Port in under 20 minutes, fully laden. An ingenious feature of the barges was the funnel, designed to that it could be lowered as the barge travelled under the Liffey bridges at high tide.

The last barge sailed down the Liffey on 21 June 1961.

The ships

Ships played a central part in the export of Guinness beer around the world. The first ship owned by the brewery was the *W. M. Barkley*, bought second-hand in 1913. It was torpedoed and sunk off the coast of Ireland by a German U-boat in 1917.

The *Clareisland* and *Clarecastle* were acquired next and in 1931 the SS *Guinness* was built at Troon, in Scotland. From 1952, when the MV *Lady Grania* was built, all Guinness Company ships were named after women in the Guinness family.

In 1977 the MV *Miranda Guinness*, the last of the Guinness Company ships to be built, made her maiden voyage. She was the world's first specially commissioned bulk-liquid carrier.

ABOVE Two barges, Castleknock *and* Killiney, *moored side by side at Dublin Port. Moored behind them is MV* Lady Grania.

World travellers

In the 1800s the Guinness Company empire expanded and Guinness was exported to many overseas markets, from Australia to Uruguay.

Crossing the equator

One of the problems with this, though, lay in the fact that the beer was exported in casks and then bottled and sold by agents when it arrived at its destination. This meant that the brewery at St James's Gate had no control over how the beer was labelled and sold, and, more importantly, no knowledge of possible forgeries: lesser beers being sold as Guinness.

They also didn't know what effect long sea voyages were having on the beer and what the beer actually tasted like when it reached its customers. Of all the Guinness exported around the world, the journey that was considered most detrimental to the quality of the beer was the voyage from Dublin to San Francisco. This involved crossing the equator and rounding Cape Horn before crossing the equator again, subjecting the beer to extreme fluctuations in temperature: cold, hot, cold and, finally, hot again.

To standardize practices and to check on quality control, the Guinness Company appointed men to travel the world to wherever their beer was sold, in order to report back their observations about each market.

Around the world and back again

Perhaps the most famous of these 'world travellers', as they were known, was Arthur T Shand, who was employed in 1898 and spent 15 years travelling the world on behalf of the company. His reports covered Australia, New Zealand, South Africa, South America, the West Indies and Canada.

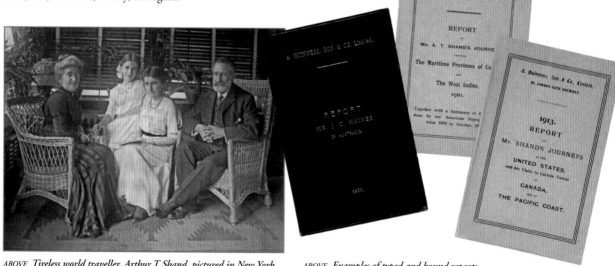

ABOVE Tireless world traveller, Arthur T Shand, pictured in New York with his wife and daughters in approximately 1910.

ABOVE Examples of typed and bound reports by Guinness 'world travellers'.

ABOVE Front cover of a 1950s booklet to advertise Guinness stout overseas.

The trips that the world travellers embarked on were lengthy. For example, one journey to South Africa undertaken by Shand in 1904 involved 80 days travelling around the country, plus the ship voyage there and back, and he covered a total distance of nearly 25,749 km (16,000 miles).

The world travellers' reports included observations on social conditions, climate and local drinking habits, but they concentrated on all matters to do with Guinness: the quality, sales, price, bottlers, agents and competition from other brands. Their handwritten reports were sent by sea back to Dublin, where they were typed and presented to the Guinness board of directors.

Ice cold

Guinness travelled to some far-flung parts of the globe, including a few places not visited by the world travellers. Sir Douglas Mawson, the great Australian explorer, took bottles of it to the Antarctic in 1911, which weathered the adverse conditions amazingly well, as explained by the member of a later expedition team that returned to the area in 1929.

Message in a bottle

In 1954, in a unique publicity exercise based on the classic 'message in a bottle' idea, the Guinness Company dropped 50,000 bottles into the sea at 11 different locations in the Atlantic, Pacific and Indian Oceans.

Each bottle contained a rolled-up booklet of facts about the beer and a numbered document claiming that the bottle drop was to aid research into the perfect way to seal a bottle. A note addressed to those who found the bottles invited them to fill in the form and send it to the Guinness Brewery. The people who responded were then sent details of where their particular bottle had been dropped, together with a gold-coloured leprechaun charm.

The bicentenary bottle drop

To mark the Guinness Company's bicentenary in 1959, there was another bottle drop but this time on an even greater scale: 150,000 specially designed Guinness bottles were dropped into the mid-Atlantic from 38 ships.

These bottles contained a certificate 'from the office of King Neptune', a gold bicentenary Guinness label, a note about the shipping line involved in dropping the bottle and instructions on how to turn the bottle into a table lamp!

About three months after the 1954 bottle drop, the first bottle was found in the Azores and soon letters began arriving at the Guinness Company offices from all over the world, from the Philippines to South America. And now, 50 years after the 1959 bottle drop, bottles are still being discovered at a rate of one or two a year. Recent finds have been reported from Canada, USA, France, South Africa and the Arctic Circle.

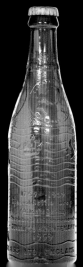

Chancing upon a bottle

Many of the people who discovered bottles from the 1954 and 1959 bottledrops wrote to the Brewery.

I was walking along the isolated beach south of the Mundrabilla Road House when I found your bottle. Myself and all the people of Mundrabilla (all five of them) love Guinness.
Geoff Peart, Gibson, Western Australia

This was our first trip to the Arctic... while walking along the beach at Coates Island I discovered two bottles which contained scrolls. My wife and I enjoy walking on beaches and over the years we have found a lot of different things but the two bottles found [in] the Arctic surely tops the lot.
Raymond McNair, New Brunswick, Canada

Myself and my partner do appreciate and enjoy a pint of your famous stout very often.
Michael O'Sullivan, Lighthouse Keeper, Dingle, Co Kerry, Ireland

Recently I experienced one of the greatest thrills when I found a bottle on the shore of one of the very romantic islands in the Bahamas and, on opening it, discovered my trophy consisted of a scroll commemorating the occasion... I read the interesting literature enclosed with your letter. I am reciprocating in turn by sending you literature descriptive of the products we manufacture.
Chester C Cooley, President, Da-Lite Screen Co, Chicago, USA

I don't [know] what the memento you mention is, but I wonder if you could rise to a second one for the school? PS Do you throw any full bottles overboard?
F M Collett, Headteacher, Tarpiem Bay School, Bahamas

Dear Sirs, I take the liberty of sending you this letter to inform you with all respect that finding myself at work, stone-breaking at the edge of the beach in this prison where I unfortunately find myself at the moment, I saw floating on the water a bottle which contained a parchment… I therefore ask you very kindly to be good enough to help me within the limit of possibility.
Name unknown, Isla Ma Madre, Nayarit, Mexico

It is very seldom that anything of such interest occurs here in Recife, except when a British ship is in port and one gets the chance of having a good old glass of Guinness.
A E Wootton, Recife, Brazil

LEFT A bottle from the 1959 bottle drop, [containing a] rolled-up certificate.

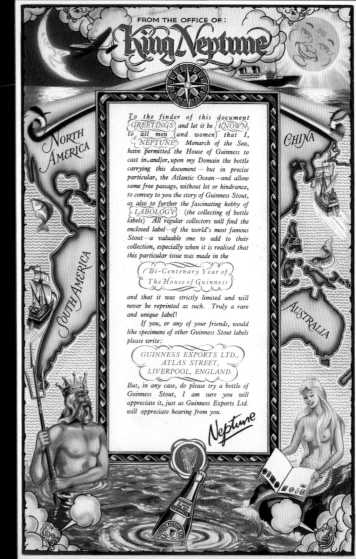

The harp

The most widely recognized symbol of Guinness is the harp. It is one of the three elements that make up the livery; the other two are the word 'Guinness' and Arthur Guinness's signature.

Trademark

Chosen by Benjamin Lee Guinness to be the company emblem, the harp was used on the first bottle label created for the Guinness Company in 1862. It was registered as a Guinness trademark in 1876.

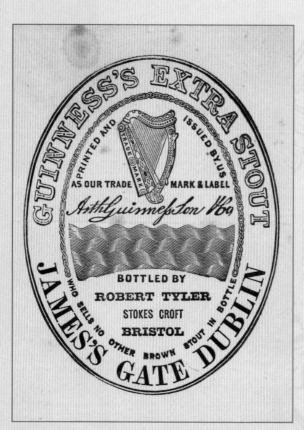

ABOVE A printer's proof of the original 1862 label shows the Brian Boru harp, together with the word Guinness and Arthur Guinness's signature.

Heraldic heritage

The harp is based on the famous 14th-century harp known as the O'Neill or Brian Boru harp, which is preserved in the library at Trinity College in Dublin. Brian Boru was the High King of Ireland from 1002 to 1014 and the harp has long been Ireland's heraldic symbol. The Cláirseach (or Gaelic) harp was used on Irish coinage by King John and King Edward I in the 13th century.

The harp is the official national emblem of the Republic of Ireland and appears on the Republic's coins, passports and official documents of state. It also appears in the official seals of the President, Taoiseach, Tánaiste, Government Ministers and other officials.

What distinguishes the harp of the national emblem from the Guinness Company harp is that the latter always appears with its straight edge – the sound board – to the left and the harp of the Republic of Ireland is always depicted with the straight edge to the right. This is because the Guinness Company registered the harp as a trademark in 1876 and nearly 50 years later, in 1922, when the newly established Irish Free State government chose to use the harp as the symbol of Ireland, they needed to distinguish it from the harp that was the emblem of the Guinness Company.

Design evolution

The design of the harp has evolved over the years and there have been several changes, including a reduction in the number of strings shown.

Harp from first trademark label, 1862.

Ornamental harp used on trademark label, 1955.

Simplified harp introduced in 1968.

Harp from trademark label, 1995.

Harp from redesigned brand identity, 1997.

Harp from redesigned brand identity, 2005.

THE BEER

What's in it?

Fans of Guinness stout often wonder what goes into it to create that famous colour and taste. Guinness is a dry stout and has just four ingredients – barley, hops, water and yeast – but it is the combination of these ingredients and the art, science and craft of the Guinness brewers that ensure the incomparable taste and look of Guinness is always a wonderful experience.

Barley

Guinness is brewed with a mix of malted, unmalted and roasted barley. The malted barley gives the beer body and goodness and contributes to the sweet malty flavours. The roasted barley is added to give Guinness its unique ruby red colour and adds to the beer's distinctive flavour.

Hops

A higher proportion of hops is used to make Guinness than to make ales or lagers. This gives Guinness a bitter flavour that balances the sweetness and roasted taste of the malt.

Hops act as a natural preservative, which in the past would have been a key component in enabling Guinness to be shipped all over the world.

'A porter brewer buys none but the best,
as none else will answer.'

Arthur Guinness

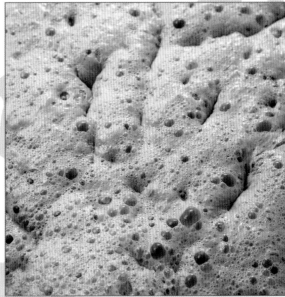

Water

The water in Guinness doesn't come from the River Liffey, as many people think, but from springs in the Wicklow Mountains, about 16 km (10 miles) south of Dublin.

The water used in brewing Guinness is very important. A pure source like the Wicklow Mountain springs provides water with a low mineral content, which allows the flavours of Guinness to come into their own.

Yeast

Yeast is added to the sweet, hopped wort and starts the fermentation process, converting the natural sugars in the grain to alcohol and carbon dioxide. The fundamental characteristics of flavour also develop during fermentation.

The yeast used to brew Guinness is considered so valuable that a special reserve culture is kept locked away, in case anything happens to the main supply.

How's it made?

Although brewing methods are constantly updated to keep pace with technological advances, Guinness is still brewed using the same fundamental processes that were used in Arthur Guinness's time.

Roast

The St James's Gate Brewery has two gigantic roasters, which heat the barley using hot air. The barley is roasted to a special set of specifications but the readiness of the roasted barley must still be assessed by the brewers to ensure the correct colour and consistency has been achieved. After roasting the barley is doused with water, cooled and stored in silos.

Mill

Malted, unmalted and roasted barley must be milled. The barley is fed from storage silos into mills in the Brewhouse, where it is crushed by a series of rollers. This releases the inner goodness and keeps the outer husk intact.

Once the barley has been milled it is called grist. The phrase 'grist for the mill' has its origins in this process.

Mash

The grist then goes through a Steele's Masher, a horizontal cylinder with a series of rotating paddles inside. As the grist passes through the paddles it is mixed with hot water, which is known as liquor. The resulting mixture, which looks like porridge, is called mash. It is stirred slowly until the malt has been converted to brewing sugars. When this process is complete, the mash is transferred into a kieve, which acts like a giant sieve. The kieve has a false bottom with slotted plates that hold back the spent grain and allow the liquid to flow through. This liquid, now called wort, is passed into a large kettle for the next stage.

Boil

The hops are added to the kettle and the mixture boiled at 100°C (212°F) for approximately 90 minutes to extract as much flavour as possible. The wort is then left to settle, before being emptied from the kettle and passed through a cooler. So far the process has taken 11 hours. The wort now leaves the Brewhouse and flows to the Fermentation and Beer Processing Plant (the FBPP).

ABOVE *The inside of Cooke's Lane Maltings, 1948.*

OPPOSITE, CLOCKWISE FROM TOP LEFT *Cleaning out spent hops from a hopback, 1948; modern brewhouse interior; wort being 'struck off' from a copper, 1948; inspection of copper no.9 in brewhouse, 1948.*

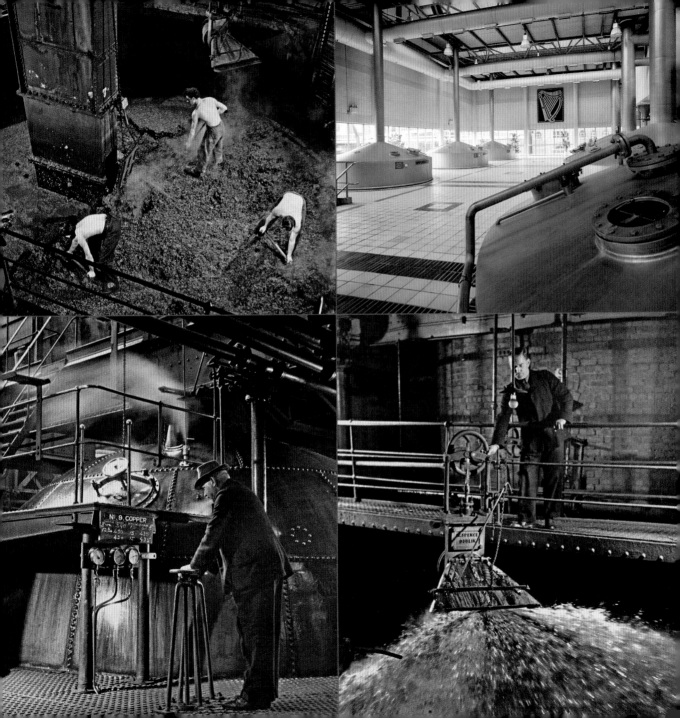

Ferment

At the Fermentation and Beer Processing Plant, the yeast is added to the wort, which then collects in a large fermentation vessel.

Microscopic yeast organisms feed on the sugars in the wort, and as they do, they produce alcohol and carbon dioxide. During fermentation the yeast rises to the top of the wort. When fermentation is finished, the yeast is separated from the beer. In the past this was done by skimming it off with a large board, but now it is achieved using centrifuges.

Mature

At this stage the beer is moved to a maturation vessel where it is allowed to settle and the unique Guinness flavour develops. Throughout the process the beer has been repeatedly tested and checked by the Quality Assurance team. It is finally assessed by the 'taste panel' before it is officially released for packaging as Guinness.

Dispatch

The beer flows to the Tank Station, where it is put into road tankers to be sent for bottling or canning, or to the Keg Plant, where the Guinness Draught kegs are washed, sterilized and filled.

RIGHT View looking up at modern stainless steel brewing vessels.

ABOVE RIGHT Yeast vessels in the fermentation plant at St James's Gate.

OPPOSITE, CLOCKWISE FROM TOP LEFT Wooden vats, 1948; filling casks of Guinness stout, circa 1906; modern road tankers; keg carousel in modern keg plant.

The people who make it

Arthur Guinness was the first in a long line of Guinness brewers, the men responsible for making the all-important beer.

The brewers

In the 1800s most brewers employed were relatives of the Guinnesses or were members of one family, the Purser family, and the traditional craft of brewing was handed down from one generation to another. Brewers were both feared and respected by the rest of the workforce.

The most senior of the brewers was the head brewer, who supervised all the other brewers and personally oversaw all aspects of the brewing process, from buying raw materials to the welfare of employees. He was held in the same high esteem as Guinness family members and was considered as important to the company as the beer that he brewed.

The epitome of gentlemanly refinement, wearing their bowler hats in the winter and straw boaters in summer, brewers enjoyed many special privileges. They had six weeks' holiday a year and began the early shift at the brewery at 7 am, an hour after the rest of the workers had begun. They had their own private dining room at the brewery site and lived in company houses where they were looked after by a housekeeper. They also had a special position in Dublin society and were considered to be very eligible bachelors.

Up until the end of the 19th century brewing was more of an art than a science. In the 1890s the Guinness Company began to approach brewing in a more scientific way and started to recruit science graduates from Oxford and Cambridge Universities.

21st-century brewing

Modern-day qualifications to become a brewer are a degree in one of the sciences plus several years of on-the-job training. The challenge of brewing these days is to marry the heritage of hundreds of years of brewing with what science and technology have to offer.

Now a multi-disciplinary team, together with sophisticated computer and automation technology, is responsible for producing about 1¾ million litres (over 3 million pints) of Guinness a day at St James's Gate. The final quality check is made by the brewers, who gather each day to taste the beer to ensure it is as good as it can be. As a marker of quality, Master Brewer Fergal Murray always asks himself if Arthur Guinness would be happy with the beer.

ABOVE *Head brewer D O Williams sampling the brew in the Brewhouse, 1960.*

'The most enjoyable part of a brewer's day is to sample his creation.'

Fergal Murray, Master Brewer

ABOVE *A brewer sampling the beer in 1948.*

INSET LEFT *Fergal Murray, current Master Brewer.*

INSET RIGHT *Just as is done today, a brewer in 1948 checks the beer kegged the previous day.*

Guinness is available around the world in a number of different variants and is delivered to drinkers in cans, bottles and on tap.

Foreign Extra Stout
Launched 1801

With extra hops to give it a distinctive taste and a longer shelf life in hot weather, this is brewed in Africa, Asia and the Caribbean, and is also available in the United Kingdom, Ireland and Italy. Foreign Extra Stout makes up 40 per cent of all the Guinness brewed around the world.

Guinness Extra Stout
Launched 1821

Extra stout was first sold in corked, stoneware bottles. Imprinted in each bottle was the name of the independent bottler (see pages 48–49). In 1834, the change was made to glass bottles, which evolved over the years into the bottles we know today.

Extra Stout Cans and Bottles

Extra stout, which now comes in cans and bottles, is a more full-bodied beer with a deeper characteristic roasted bitterness and a rich, mature texture. Of all the types of Guinness available today, this is the closest to the porter originally brewed by Arthur Guinness.

*Guinness beer may appear black, but
it is actually a very dark shade of ruby.*

Guinness Draught

Launched 1959

The iconic beer with the smooth taste that has a creamy head generated by the release of nitrogen bubbles. It has a sweet malt flavour, finished with a dry roasted taste and hoppy bitterness.

Draught Cans and Bottles

Launched Cans 1988, Bottles 1999

With the invention of the widget, Guinness Draught became portable and is available in cans and bottles.

The widget The product of decades of research and over £5 million of investment, the widget was the revolutionary invention that meant that Guinness drinkers could enjoy a pint at home that was as good as one in the pub.

First used in cans of Guinness in 1988, the widget won The Queen's Award for Technological Achievement in 1991 – a first for any brewing company. In 1999 bottled Guinness Draught was introduced with a bullet-shaped 'rocket widget' inside the bottle.

The small, plastic device is a hollow sphere about 3 cm (1¼ inches) in diameter that rests in the can or bottle until it is opened. On opening, the pressure drops and the widget floats and jets nitrogen through the beer, creating a surge and producing a long-lasting, creamy head.

The perfect pint

The best temperature at which to drink your beer is 6°C (42.8°F) and there are particular steps in the rituals both of serving and of enjoying the perfect pint.

How to pour it

Select a clean, dry, branded glass. Hold the glass firmly and put your finger on the harp symbol.

Now for the perfect pour. Take the glass and tilt it at a 45-degree angle under the spout. Grab hold of the tap and, pulling the handle slowly towards you in a smooth motion, allow the beer to flow steadily down the side of the glass.

Straighten the glass up, bringing the flow of beer up towards the top of the harp symbol on the glass, and – slowly and evenly – come to a stop.

Put the glass down and allow the beer to settle. There is a cascade and surge as the nitrogen bubbles form the creamy head at the top of the beer. Allow the head to form as the foundation for the next step: the top up.

Now for the second part of the two-part pour. Pick the glass up again and hold it straight under the tap. To create the head, push the handle away from you slightly and let the beer flow in slowly until the head is proud of the rim of the glass. Close the tap.

It takes 119.5 seconds to pour the perfect pint.

And how to drink it

Pick your glass up. Raise your arm and hold your elbow out at a 90-degree angle from your body so that you can look through the horizon of the glass and not down at it.

Now bring the glass up to your lips, rather than bending your head down to the glass. Take a mouthful and taste the three distinct parts of the beer: the sweetness of the malt on your tongue, the roasted flavour at the sides of your mouth and the bitterness at the back of your throat.

You should always drink from the same side of the glass and aim to keep the head on the beer a constant size, right to the end. The head will form lacy rings on the side of the glass and you can – if you like – count them to see how many sips you have had. Cheers!

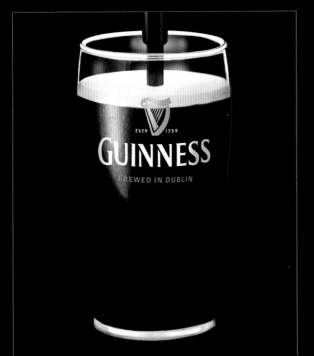

Global Guinness

After more than a century of shipping beer around the world, the Guinness Company began to brew beer overseas. The first brewery outside Ireland was opened in London in 1936.

A brewery was opened in Ikeja, Nigeria in 1963 – the first Guinness brewery to be built overseas. A second overseas brewery was built near Kuala Lumpur in Malaysia three years later and Guinness breweries subsequently opened in Cameroon in 1970 and Ghana in 1971. Alongside these breweries, the Guinness Company established contracts with other brewers around the globe to brew Guinness beer under licence.

In 1991 the Guinness Company set up brewing agreements with breweries in Jamaica, Barbados, Burkina Faso, Congo, Gabon, Guyana and Tanzania, and a few years later in Vietnam. And so it continued until today, when Guinness is brewed in 48 countries around the world. Nigeria – home of the first overseas brewery – has grown to be the third largest market for Guinness, after Ireland and the United Kingdom.

BELOW 'The world and his wife' booklet advertising Guinness stout overseas, 1960s.

10 million glasses of Guinness are enjoyed every day in over 150 countries around the world.

GUINNESS AVAILABLE HERE

- Andorra
- Angola
- Anguilla
- Antigua 🍺
- Argentina
- Aruba
- Australia 🍺
- Austria
- Azerbaijan

- Bahamas 🍺
- Bahrain
- Barbados 🍺
- Belarus
- Belgium
- Belize 🍺
- Benin 🍺
- Bermuda
- Bonaire
- Bosnia and
  Herzegovina
- Botswana
- Brazil
- Bulgaria
- Burkina Faso 🍺

- Cambodia
- Cameroon 🍺
- Canada 🍺
- Canary Islands
- Cayman Islands
- Central African
  Republic 🍺
- Chad
- Channel Islands
- Chile
- China
- Costa Rica
- Croatia
- Cuba
- Curaçao
- Cyprus
- Czech Republic

🍺 = Guinness brewed here

- Democratic
  Republic
  of Congo 🍺
- Denmark
- Dominica 🍺

- Egypt
- El Salvador
- Equatorial Guinea
- Estonia
- Ethiopia

- Falkland Islands
- Fiji
- Finland
- France
- French Guiana

- Gabon 🍺
- Gambia 🍺
- Georgia
- Germany
- Ghana 🍺
- Gibraltar
- Greece
- Grenada 🍺
- Guadeloupe
- Guinea 🍺
- Guinea-Bissau
- Guyana 🍺

- Haiti 🍺
- Hong Kong
- Hungary

- Iceland
- India
- Indonesia 🍺
- Iran
- Ireland 🍺
- Israel
- Italy
- Ivory Coast 🍺

- Jamaica 🍺
- Japan
- Jordan

- Kazakhstan
- Kenya 🍺

- Latvia
- Lebanon
- Lesotho
- Liberia 🍺
- Liechtenstein
- Lithuania
- Luxembourg

- Macau
- Malaysia 🍺
- Maldives
- Mali 🍺
- Malta
- Martinique
- Mauritius 🍺
- Mexico
- Monaco
- Montserrat
- Morocco

- Namibia
- Nepal
- The Netherlands
- New Caledonia

- New Zealand 🍺
- Nigeria 🍺
- Norway

- Oman

- Panama 🍺
- The Philippines
- Poland
- Portugal
- Puerto Rico

- Qatar

- Réunion
- Romania
- Russia 🍺
- Rwanda 🍺

- Saba
- St Barthélemy
- St Eustatius
- St Kitts and
  Nevis 🍺
- St Lucia 🍺
- St Maarten
- St Vincent and
  The Grenadines 🍺
- San Marino
- Serbia and
  Montenegro
- Seychelles 🍺
- Sierra Leone 🍺
- Singapore 🍺
- Slovakia
- Slovenia
- South Africa
- South Korea
- Spain
- Sri Lanka
- Suriname
- Swaziland
- Sweden
- Switzerland
- Syria

- Taiwan
- Tanzania 🍺
- Thailand
- Togo 🍺
- Trinidad and
  Tobago 🍺
- Tunisia
- Turkey
- Turks and Caicos
  Islands

- Uganda 🍺
- Ukraine
- United Arab
  Emirates
- United Kingdom
- United States
  of America
- Uruguay
- U.S. Virgin Islands

- Vietnam

- Yemen

- Zambia
- Zimbabwe

GUINNESS EN EUROPA

VENECIA

The world and his wife enjoy Guinness

There's nothing like a **GUINNESS**

The labels

Until the 20th century Guinness was brewed at St James's Gate, but it wasn't bottled there. Instead it was sent in bulk to independent bottlers, most of whom labelled the bottles of beer with labels bearing their own trademark, often depicting animals. As well as bottling the beer, these bottlers were responsible for distributing and marketing it overseas.

THE ADS

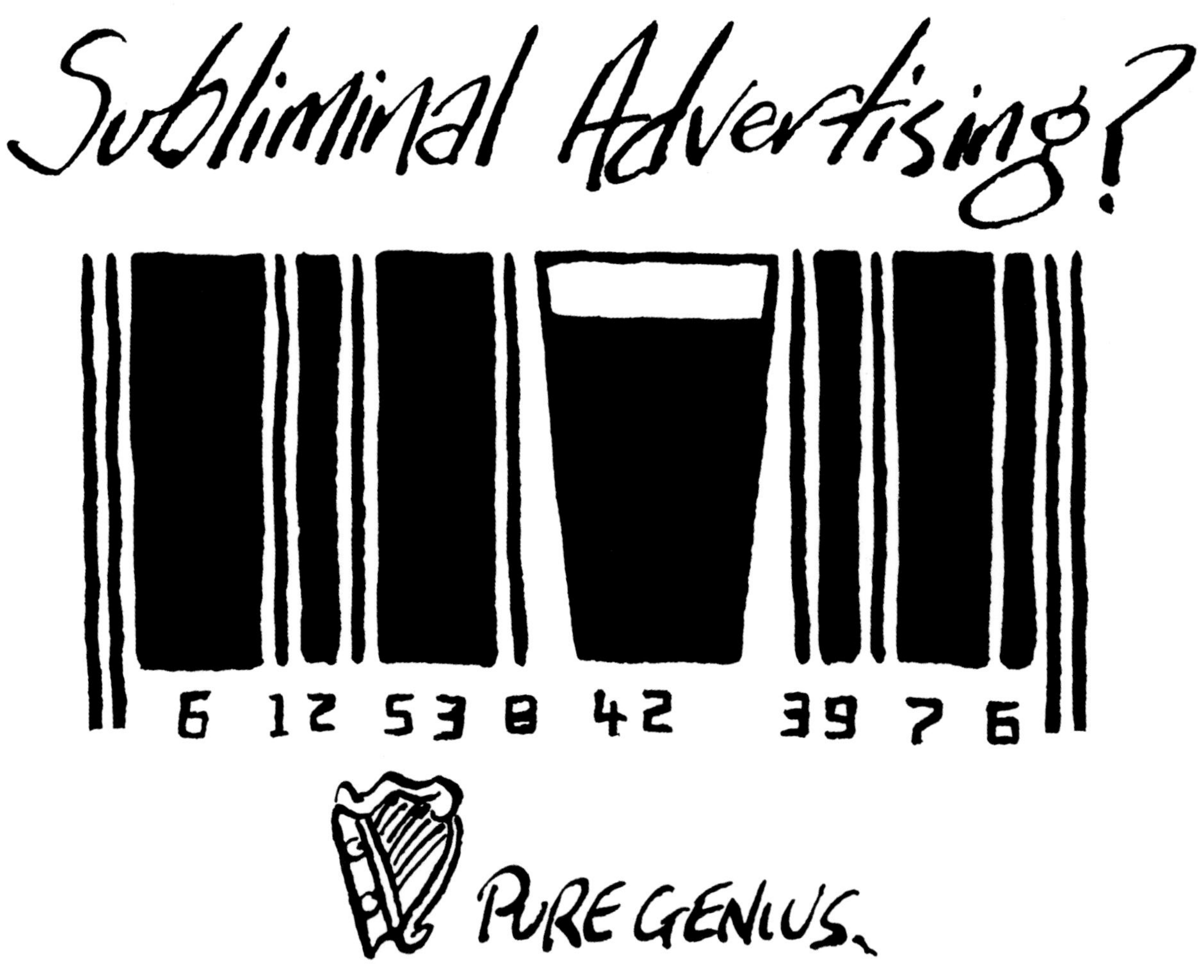
Subliminal Advertising?
6 12 538 42 3976
PURE GENIUS.

health-giving properties, this simple message became one of the most well-known slogans in advertising history. This claim is naturally not one that the Guinness Company would endorse now.

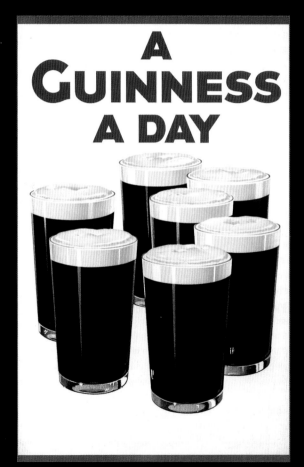

1932

1938

UNMISTAKABLE

Guinness
IS GOOD FOR YOU

1930s

1931

1947

430

Drawing by J. Gilroy

G.E.1346

As the New Gnu knew
very soon at the Zoo
Guinness is good for you

1946

Keep Guinness Time

GUINNESS

5 MILLION GUINNESS ARE ENJOYED EVERY DAY

1961

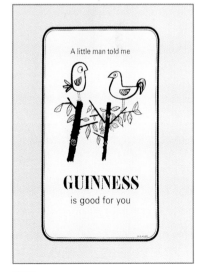

A little man told me

GUINNESS
is good for you

1966

GUINNESS TIME

Have this one with me !

1934

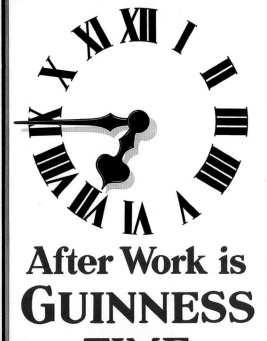

After Work is
**GUINNESS
TIME**
GUINNESS IS GOOD FOR YOU

1931

Ten to one it's
**GUINNESS
TIME**

1931

1951

1956

1936

1958

Guinness for strength

The celebrated poster of a man carrying a girder from this series of adverts was so popular that people began asking for a 'girder' when they wanted a Guinness in pubs. Beginning in the 1930s, the campaign, the work of the gifted John Gilroy, made regular appearances until the middle of the 1960s.

60

THE ADS

1934

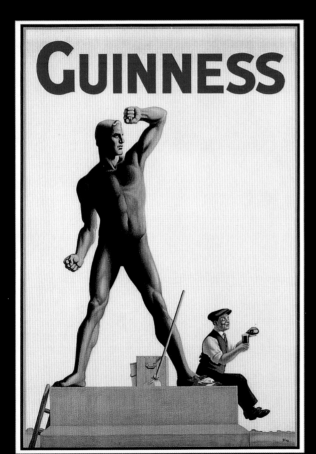

1937

1945

1945

1949

1951

menagerie of charming animals that steal his beer. These animals captured the imagination of the public and the posters are among the best-known graphic art of the 20th century. Although the slogan was mainly associated with the animals, it was also used on other posters depicting bottles of Guinness being threatened by some calamity or another.

1935

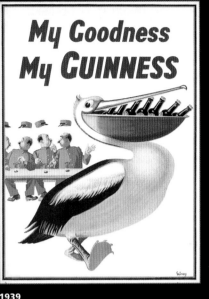

1936

My Goodness

My GUINNESS

1943

1949

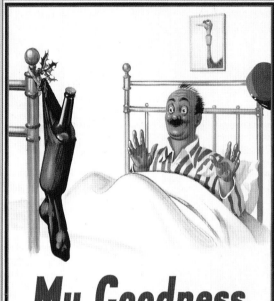

**My Goodness
My Christmas
GUINNESS**

1937

**My Goodness
My GUINNESS**

1938

The toucan

The iconic Guinness toucan actually began life as a pelican, but advertising copywriter Dorothy L Sayers – later to become famous as the author of the Lord Peter Wimsey crime novels – changed 'pelican' to 'toucan', as this rhymed with more words. John Gilroy developed the popular character and it appeared in advertisements for Guinness for several decades.

1953

If he can say as you can
Guinness is good for you
How grand to be a Toucan
Just think what Toucan do

1935

1955

Love

ly day for a
GUINNESS

Other classics

Alongside the big campaigns, over many decades there have been other press adverts and posters that highlighted the creativity and innovation of Guinness advertising. Here are just a few favourites.

1955

1956

5 MILLION GUINNESS

for strength every day

1958

GUINNESS NONSCIENCE

1960

after work
GUINNESS

ECKERSLEY

1961

GOODNESS!
GUINNESS!

R.PEPPÉ

1962

1953

Genius

The idea behind this campaign from the agency Ogilvy and Mather, which combined the 'genius' of the people who made Guinness with the 'genius' of the people who drank it, was so strong that the Chief Executive of Guinness made an on-the-spot decision to run with it when the idea was presented.

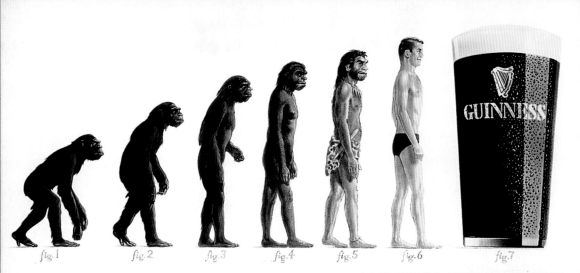

GUINNESS. PURE GENIUS.

1985

TWO HEADS ARE BETTER THAN ONE

GUINNESS. PURE GENIUS.

1987

COOL GUINNESS. PURE GENIUS.

1987

THE AUSTRALIAN FOR GENIUS

GUINNESS

GUINNESS. PURE GENIUS.

1985

'*Guinness is not just an advertising icon; in Britain it is the advertising icon…arguably the brand of the century.*'

Stefano Hatfield, *Campaign*, 16 January 1998

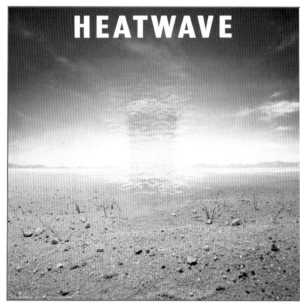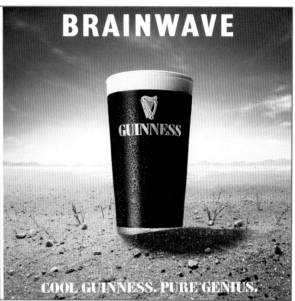

1987

Fractionals

'Fractionals' was linked to the successful television campaign, 'The Man with the Guinness' from the 1980s and '90s. The posters – supposedly the scribbled musings of 'The Man with the Guinness' – had a very individual tone.

1991

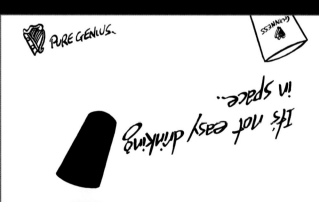

1992

You're staring again.

1992

Temporary colour-
blindness.

PURE GENIUS.

1994

Me on the 'Leaning
Tower of Pisa.'

PURE GENIUS.

1992

THE FOOD

Gastronomic Guinness

Guinness stout has been part of Irish food traditions for generations, either added to dishes as an integral ingredient or enjoyed as a fitting accompaniment to many different meals.

Add a drop of the black stuff

Some might take a bit of persuading that pouring a perfectly good pint into a saucepan, rather than simply drinking it, is a good use of beer, but the results are worth it.

Guinness stout is traditionally added to hearty, homemade dishes such as chunky soups and warming winter stews, particularly Guinness and beef stew, a recipe for which every family and every pub in Ireland has its own version. The affinity of the beer with seafood, such as mussels, lobster and fish, is a long-lived one and incorporating Guinness into the batter for fried fish will give light and crisp results. Dense, rich fruit cakes, just like grandma used to make, will also benefit from a dash of the beer, which adds moistness and depth of flavour.

Try it with...

Guinness works well as an accompaniment to many types of food, too. The combination of a pint of Guinness and a serving of oysters is the classic choice and it is excellent with all seafood: the salty flavours are enhanced by the roasted bitterness of the stout. It is also a perfect partner for more surprising food favourites, such as rich desserts and sharp cheeses.

Guinness Draught is good drunk as an accompaniment to chocolate, especially dark chocolate, as it has a hint of caramel sweetness. A glass of Extra Stout works well with spicy dishes and seafood, particularly smoked salmon. Foreign Extra Stout has extra hops which gives the beer some floral overtones that particularly complement chicken and other white meat.

1940s

'I supped at the Carlton, with a large party, off oysters and Guinness, and got to bed at half-past twelve o'clock. Thus, ended the most remarkable day hitherto of my life.'

Benjamin Disraeli, Prime Minister of the United Kingdom, 1837

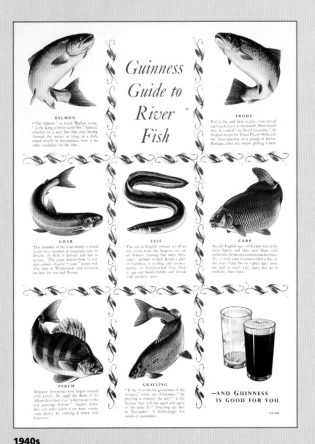

1940s

1940s

Irish rarebit

Cheese on toast is everybody's favourite,
and this version has a real bite!

THE FOOD

Preparation time 5 minutes
Cooking time 10 minutes
Serves 4

50 ml (2 fl oz) draught **GUINNESS**
1 teaspoon **Worcestershire sauce**
1 teaspoon **Dijon mustard**
1 teaspoon **English mustard powder**
good pinch of **cayenne pepper**
1 **free-range egg**, beaten
200 g (7 oz) **mature Irish Cheddar cheese**, grated
4 slices of good **rustic bread**
paprika, for dusting
mixed **salad leaves** or **watercress**, to serve

step 1 Put the Guinness, Worcestershire sauce, mustards and cayenne pepper in a saucepan and bring to a simmer, stirring to dissolve any lumps. Remove the pan from the heat. Stir in the egg and cheese together, a little at a time, until you have the consistency of thick porridge.

step 2 Toast the bread slices lightly on one side under a preheated medium grill. Spoon and then spread the cheese mixture over the untoasted sides. Dust lightly with paprika.

step 3 Return the rarebits to the grill and cook until the cheese is bubbling and flecked golden brown. Serve each slice topped with a handful of mixed salad leaves or watercress.

Galway oyster bisque

A festival of flavours, this velvety, creamy soup will bring
a touch of luxury to any dinner party.

THE FOOD

Preparation time 20 minutes
Cooking time 25 minutes
Serves 4

28 **oysters**
200 ml (7 fl oz) **fish stock**
1 **onion**, diced
2 **celery sticks**, diced
150 g (5 oz) **potato**, diced
150 ml (¼ pint) draught **GUINNESS**
pinch of freshly grated **nutmeg**
a few **saffron threads**
¼ teaspoon **celery salt**
¼ teaspoon **cayenne pepper**
200 ml (7 fl oz) **double cream**

To garnish
paprika

step 1 Working over a bowl to catch the
juices, hold each oyster in turn flat-
side up. Insert an oyster knife
between the shells just to one side
of the hinged end. Twist the knife
until the shells loosen. Run the
knife inside the top shell to
release completely and then
discard the shell. Run the knife
under the oyster to loosen
from the bottom shell and
remove the flesh.

step 2 Roughly chop the flesh, reserving 8 whole oysters. Strain the reserved
oyster juices through a fine-mesh sieve or a sieve lined with muslin to
eliminate any tiny pieces of shell.

step 3 Put the strained oyster juices and stock in a saucepan and add the
onion, celery, potato and Guinness. Bring to the boil, then reduce the
heat, cover and simmer for 15 minutes until all the vegetables are
softened. Leave to cool slightly, then stir in the chopped oysters.
Transfer to a food processor and process to a purée.

step 4 Return the purée to the pan and add the nutmeg, saffron, celery
salt, cayenne pepper and cream. Heat over a medium heat for
2–3 minutes. Remove from the heat and stir in the reserved whole
oysters to warm through.

step 5 Ladle the bisque into warmed serving bowls with two oysters in each
and serve, garnished with a dusting of paprika and accompanied with
Guinness caraway bread (see pages 100–101), if liked.

Guinness, shallot and blue cheese pâté

A delicious lunch, an easy starter or even better served with walnuts and grapes at the end of a meal.

Preparation time 15 minutes, plus chilling
Cooking time 5 minutes
Serves 6

50 g (2 oz) **unsalted butter**
1 **shallot**, finely chopped
100 ml (3½ fl oz) draught **GUINNESS**
finely pared **zest** of ½ **lemon**
200 g (7 oz) **Cashel Blue** or mature **Stilton cheese**, crumbled
125 g (4 oz) **soft cream cheese**
¼ teaspoon **ground nutmeg**
1 tablespoon chopped **flat leaf parsley**
pepper
warm **toasted soldiers**, to serve

step 1 Melt the butter in a saucepan, add the shallot and cook gently for 5 minutes until softened. Remove the pan from the heat, pour in the Guinness and stir well.

step 2 Put the remaining ingredients in a food processor, season with plenty of pepper and then add the Guinness and shallot mixture. Process to a smooth paste. Divide the mixture between 6 individual ramekins.

step 3 Cover the pâtes and chill in the refrigerator for 2 hours. Allow to return to room temperature before serving with warm toasted soldiers.

Guinness crêpes with creamy wild mushrooms

Wild mushrooms give a wonderful flavour and texture
to the filling of these crispy crêpes.

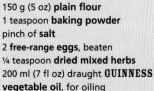

Preparation time 10 minutes
Cooking time 35–45 minutes
Serves 4

Crêpes
150 g (5 oz) **plain flour**
1 teaspoon **baking powder**
pinch of **salt**
2 **free-range eggs**, beaten
¼ teaspoon **dried mixed herbs**
200 ml (7 fl oz) draught GUINNESS
vegetable oil, for oiling

Filling
25 g (1 oz) **butter**
750 g (1½ lb) **mixed wild and field
    mushrooms**, broken into small chunks
125 ml (4 fl oz) **crème fraîche**
½ teaspoon **dark soy sauce**
pepper

step 1 Sift the flour, baking powder and salt together into a bowl. Add the eggs, herbs and Guinness to a well in the centre of the flour and gradually beat in until you have a smooth batter.

step 2 Pour a small amount of oil into a nonstick pan and tilt to coat the base, then wipe away any excess with a wad of kitchen paper. Heat over a medium to high heat and add about 3 tablespoons of the batter, swirling it around immediately to coat the base, to make a thin crêpe. Cook for about 3 minutes until bubbles appear on the surface, then flip the crêpe over and cook for 1–2 minutes until the underside is browned and crisp. Remove the crêpe from the pan and keep it warm in a low oven. Repeat with the remaining batter to make 8–9 crêpes in total, re-oiling the pan when necessary.

step 3 Meanwhile, to make the filling, melt the butter in a separate frying pan, add the mushrooms and season with pepper. Cook over a medium heat for 5 minutes. Add the crème fraîche and soy sauce, increase the heat until bubbling and cook for 2–3 minutes until the sauce has reduced slightly so that it coats the mushrooms thickly.

step 4 To serve, spoon some of the creamy mushroom mixture on to one half of each crêpe and fold the other half of the crêpe over, then finish with a dessertspoonful of the mushroom mixture on top.

Guinness, red onion and Cheddar soup

A truly scrumptious soup that makes a meal in itself.
Adding Guinness gives it a real depth of flavour.

Preparation time 10 minutes
Cooking time 1 hour
Serves 6

25 g (1 oz) **butter**
2 tablespoons **olive oil**
4 large **red onions**, about 750 g (1½ lb)
   in total, quartered and sliced
2 **garlic cloves**, finely chopped
2–3 **sage leaves**, torn, plus extra whole
   leaves to garnish
leaves from 2 **thyme sprigs**
250 ml (8 fl oz) draught **GUINNESS**
1 litre (1¾ pints) **chicken stock**
2 teaspoons **Worcestershire sauce**
1 heaped tablespoon **soft dark brown
   sugar**
6 slices of slightly stale **sourdough bread**
125 g (4 oz) **Cheddar cheese**, grated
salt and **pepper**

step 1 Melt the butter with the oil in a heavy-based saucepan, add the onions, garlic and herbs and season with salt and plenty of pepper. Cover and cook over a low heat for 40 minutes until the onions are silky and translucent.

step 2 Stir in the Guinness, stock, Worcestershire sauce and sugar and bring to the boil. Reduce the heat and simmer, uncovered, for 20 minutes until the soup has reduced slightly and developed a rich, deep flavour.

step 3 Meanwhile, toast the bread slices lightly on both sides under a preheated medium grill. Using a 3.5 cm (1½ inch) biscuit cutter, cut out 2 rings of toast per serving. Pile each one with some cheese, then return to the grill and cook until the cheese has melted.

step 4 Ladle the soup into warmed bowls, float the toasted cheese rounds on top and garnish with a few sage leaves.

Iced chocolate, Guinness and orange cake

This sumptuous cake is perfect for a special occasion. The recipe may seem a little involved, but it's easy to accomplish if tackled stage by stage.

Preparation time 45 minutes
Cooking time 1 hour
Serves 8

2 large **oranges**
250 g (8 oz) **caster sugar**
175 g (6 oz) **unsalted butter**, plus extra for greasing
150 g (5 oz) **self-raising flour**
25 g (1 oz) **cocoa powder**
2 teaspoons **baking powder**
3 **free-range eggs**, beaten
25 g (1 oz) **ground almonds**
5 tablespoons draught GUINNESS
150 ml (¼ pint) **double cream**

Icing
20 g (¾ oz) **unsalted butter**
50 g (2 oz) **caster sugar**
3 tablespoons draught GUINNESS
100 g (3½ oz) **plain dark chocolate** (70% cocoa solids), finely chopped

step 1 Peel one orange. Finely grate the zest of the other orange and set aside. Using a sharp knife, pare away the pith from both oranges. Cut the oranges into 5 mm (¼ inch) slices. Put them in a small saucepan and just cover with cold water. Bring to the boil, then reduce the heat and simmer for 10 minutes. Add 50 g (2 oz) of the sugar and continue to simmer until all the liquid has boiled away, watching carefully to ensure that the oranges don't burn. Leave to cool.

step 2 Beat together the butter and the remaining sugar for the cake in a large bowl until very pale and fluffy. Sift together the flour, cocoa and baking powder, then beat into the butter mixture alternately with the eggs. Add the ground almonds, reserved grated orange zest and Guinness and beat for 3–4 minutes until you have a soft dropping consistency.

step 3 Grease and line the base and sides of 2 x 20 cm (8 inch) round cake tins, then divide the cake mixture equally between the tins, smoothing the surface. Bake the cakes in a preheated oven, 190°C (375°F), Gas Mark 5, for 25 minutes until risen and firm to the touch. Leave to cool in the tins for 5 minutes before carefully turning out on to a wire rack to cool completely.

step 4 Whip the cream in a bowl until soft peaks form, then spread over one of the cakes. Arrange the cooled orange pieces over the cream and carefully place the other cake on top.

step 5 To make the icing, put the butter, sugar and Guinness in a small saucepan. Stir over a gentle heat until the sugar has dissolved, then bring to the boil. Remove from the heat and add the chocolate. Leave to soften, then beat gently with a wooden spoon. Leave to cool and thicken. While still warm but not too runny, pour the icing over the cake and use the back of a spoon or a palette knife to spread it evenly.

Guinness caraway bread

This easy-to-make rye bread offers an ideal base for a luxury sandwich, such as sliced smoked chicken, horseradish and rocket, best enjoyed with a glass of Guinness.

Preparation time 15 minutes, plus rising
Cooking time 30 minutes
Makes 1 loaf

250 g (8 oz) **strong white flour**, plus extra for dusting
250 g (8 oz) **rye flour**
1 teaspoon **salt**
2 teaspoons **fast-action dried yeast**
2 teaspoons **caraway seeds**, plus extra for sprinkling
300 ml (½ pint) draught **GUINNESS**, plus extra if necessary
1 dessertspoon **black treacle**
vegetable oil, for oiling

step 1 Put the flours, salt, yeast and caraway seeds in a large bowl and mix together well.

step 2 Warm the Guinness in a small saucepan with the treacle, then pour into the dry ingredients. Mix to make a moist but not wet dough – you may need to add extra Guinness if the mixture looks a little dry, otherwise the yeast will not activate properly and the bread will not rise. Knead briefly on a lightly floured work surface, then cover with clingfilm and leave to rise for 2 hours in a warm place.

step 3 Knock back the dough and knead on a lightly floured work surface for 2–3 minutes. Shape into an oval loaf and place on an oiled baking sheet. Sprinkle over some extra caraway seeds. Cover lightly with a dampened clean tea towel and leave to rise for about 1 hour in a warm place.

step 4 Remove the tea towel and make 5 slashes crossways in the top of the loaf. Put the loaf in a preheated oven, 230°C (450°F), Gas Mark 8, then immediately reduce the temperature to 200°C (400°F), Gas Mark 6, and bake for 25 minutes. Check that it is cooked by tapping the bottom of the loaf – it should sound hollow. Turn out on to a wire rack and leave to cool.

Preparation time 45 minutes, plus soaking
Cooking time 2 hours
Serves 12

250 g (8 oz) **seedless raisins**
250 g (8 oz) **sultanas**
125 g (4 oz) **prunes**, stoned and chopped
330 ml (11 fl oz) bottle of **GUINNESS**
200 g (7 oz) **unsalted butter**
200 g (7 oz) **soft light brown sugar**
1 tablespoon **black treacle**
3 large **free-range eggs**
200 g (7 oz) **plain flour**, sifted
65 g (2½ oz) **ground almonds**
¼ whole **nutmeg**, freshly grated
1 teaspoon **ground cinnamon**
125 g (4 oz) good-quality **orange marmalade**
75 g (3 oz) **walnuts**, chopped

step 1 Put the raisins, sultanas and prunes in a bowl and pour over 300 ml (½ pint) of the Guinness. Cover and leave to soak overnight.

step 2 Grease and line the base and side of a 23 cm (9 inch) round cake tin with a double thickness of greaseproof paper that stands about 5 cm (2 inches) above the rim of the tin.

step 3 Beat together the butter and sugar in a bowl until very pale and fluffy. Add the treacle, eggs, flour, ground almonds and spices and beat until well combined. Cut up any large pieces of orange peel in the marmalade, then add the marmalade and walnuts to the soaked fruit. Stir into the cake mixture, which should be quite stiff in order to hold the fruit and nuts in place rather than sinking to the bottom of the cake. Tip into the prepared tin and smooth the surface.

step 4 Bake in a preheated oven, 180°C (350°F), Gas Mark 4, for 30 minutes, then reduce the temperature to 160°C (325°F), Gas Mark 3, cover lightly with a double-thickness piece of greaseproof paper and bake for a further 1½ hours, or until a skewer or thin-bladed knife inserted into the centre comes out clean.

step 5 Leave the cake to cool in the tin. Meanwhile, make holes all over the cake surface with a skewer and spoon over the remaining Guinness. When the cake is cold, remove it from the tin, strip off the lining papers and wrap first in clean greaseproof paper and then tightly in foil. Leave for at least a week before cutting.

Guinness honeycomb ice cream

No one would guess that this beautiful pale coffee-coloured ice cream contains Guinness if they did not know. Keep them guessing – it is utterly delicious.

Preparation time 30 minutes, plus freezing
Cooking time 15–25 minutes
Serves 4

6 **egg yolks**
125 g (4 oz) **light muscovado sugar**
300 ml (½ pint) **single cream**
150 ml (¼ pint) draught **GUINNESS**
2 x 40 g (2 x 1½ oz) **chocolate-covered honeycomb bars**, chopped

step 1 Put the egg yolks and sugar in a large heatproof bowl set over a saucepan of simmering water, making sure that the base of the bowl doesn't touch the water. Stir until the sugar has dissolved, then remove from the heat.

step 2 Heat the cream and Guinness in a nonstick saucepan to just below boiling point – don't worry if the mixture looks slightly curdled at this point. Pour over the egg yolk and sugar mixture, beating well with a balloon whisk.

step 3 Return the mixture to the nonstick pan and cook over the lowest possible heat, stirring constantly, until the custard starts to thicken and coats the back of the spoon. This will take at least 10 minutes and up to 20 minutes.

step 4 Pour the mixture back into the heatproof bowl and leave to cool completely, then stir in the chopped chocolate-covered honeycomb bars. Turn the ice cream into a shallow plastic container and freeze for 2 hours, then remove it from the freezer and stir well. Return to the freezer until completely frozen.

step 5 Remove the ice cream from the freezer and leave at room temperature for a few minutes to soften slightly before serving.

Guinness
goes so well with food
Menu

GUINNESS is good for you

Sweet Guinness-soaked ham with celeriac salad

This succulent Guinness-infused ham can be served hot for supper, cold for lunch or warm for the perfect ham and eggs breakfast.

Preparation time 15 minutes
Cooking time 2 hours
Serves 8–10

1 x 2 kg (4 lb) 'corner cut' **gammon joint**
1 litre (1¾ pints) draught **GUINNESS**
1 **vegetable stock cube**
1 **onion**, unpeeled and quartered
12 **black peppercorns**
2 **bay leaves**
1 tablespoon **demerara sugar**
2 tablespoons **dark molasses sugar**

Celeriac salad
1 **celeriac**, about 500 g (1 lb)
2 tablespoons **lemon juice**
2 large **green dessert apples**
8 tablespoons **mayonnaise**
2 tablespoons **white wine vinegar**
2 heaped teaspoons **Dijon mustard**
2 tablespoons chopped **parsley**
salt and **pepper**

step 1 Put the gammon joint in a suitably sized saucepan. Pour over the Guinness, crumble in the stock cube and add the onion, peppercorns, bay leaves and demerara sugar. Top up with cold water if necessary to cover the gammon. Bring to the boil, then reduce the heat to a gentle simmer and cook for 45 minutes.

step 2 Remove the joint from the pan, discarding the liquid, and wrap completely in foil, rind-side up. Place in a roasting tin and add water to a depth of 1 cm (½ inch). Roast in a preheated oven, 180°C (350°F), Gas Mark 4, for 45 minutes.

step 3 Leave the ham until cool enough to handle, then roll the foil back at the top. Using a sharp knife, remove and discard the rind, leaving the fat in place on the joint. Score the fat diagonally both ways into a diamond pattern and press the molasses sugar into the openings and all over the fat. Tuck the foil back around the meaty parts of the joint, leaving the sugary area exposed. Return the ham to the oven for 15 minutes until the coating is just crisp and golden. Leave to rest for 10 minutes before serving hot, or leave to cool for serving warm or cold.

step 4 Meanwhile, to make the salad, peel the celeriac until you have only clean, creamy flesh. Cut it into julienne strips (the size of a long matchstick), put in a non-reactive bowl and douse with the lemon juice. Peel and core the apples, then cut into similar-sized strips, add to the celeriac and mix well. In a separate bowl, combine the mayonnaise, vinegar, mustard and parsley and season well with salt and pepper. Pour over the celeriac and apples and gently mix together to coat thoroughly.

step 5 Put 2 or 3 slices of the ham on one side of each serving plate and spoon the celeriac salad on the other side, just so that the salad overlaps the edge of the ham.

Sausages with Guinness gravy and colcannon

Bangers and mash doesn't get any better than this! Guinness in gravy is a marriage made in heaven.

Preparation time 15 minutes
Cooking time 25 minutes
Serves 4

625 g (1¼ lb) **potatoes**
50 ml (2 fl oz) **milk**
65 g (2½ oz) **butter**
¼ teaspoon **English mustard powder**
pinch of freshly grated **nutmeg**
1 tablespoon **plain flour**
300 ml (½ pint) **beef stock**
125 ml (4 fl oz) draught **GUINNESS**
1 tablespoon **tomato purée**
2 teaspoons **redcurrant jelly**
½ teaspoon **dried mixed herbs**
8 good-quality **butcher's sausages**
clear honey, for brushing
75 g (3 oz) **cabbage**, finely chopped
75 g (3 oz) **leeks**, finely chopped
6 **spring onions**, chopped (including green parts)
salt and **pepper**

step 1 Cook the potatoes in a saucepan of salted boiling water until tender. Drain well, then beat into a mash, adding the milk, 25 g (1 oz) of the butter, the mustard and nutmeg and seasoning well with pepper and salt as required. Cover and keep warm.

step 2 While the potatoes are cooking, prepare the gravy. Melt 15 g (½ oz) of the butter in a saucepan, add the flour and cook over a gentle heat, stirring rapidly, for 1 minute. Add the stock, Guinness, tomato purée, jelly and herbs and bring to the boil (you may need to beat with a balloon whisk to dissolve the jelly properly). Reduce the heat and simmer for 2–3 minutes until you have a rich, textured gravy. Keep hot.

step 3 Cook the sausages under a preheated medium grill, turning frequently and brushing with a little honey, until golden all over and cooked through (about 10–15 minutes).

step 4 Meanwhile, Melt the remaining butter in a large frying pan, add the cabbage and leeks and cook for 5 minutes until soft. Add the spring onions and cook for a further 3–4 minutes. Fold into the mash to make the colcannon.

step 5 Spoon a nest of colcannon into the centre of each warmed serving plate. Nestle the sausages into the colcannon. Spoon the rich Guinness gravy around the edge and serve.

"Now, I feel I need a GUINNESS"

Pork, Guinness and potato pie

A good-looking dish featuring layers of meat, root vegetables and sliced potatoes braised in herb-infused Guinness and served with sautéed apples.

Preparation time 20 minutes
Cooking time 1¾ hours
Serves 4

vegetable oil, for oiling
2 large **waxy potatoes** (Desirée or Wilja are perfect), peeled and finely sliced
500 g (1 lb) **pork tenderloin**
1 large **onion**, finely sliced into rings
3 large **carrots**, peeled and finely sliced lengthways
1 heaped tablespoon mixed finely chopped **sage** and **parsley**
350 ml (12 fl oz) draught GUINNESS
150 ml (¼ pint) **vegetable stock**
1 tablespoon **Dijon mustard**
salt and **pepper**

Topping (optional)
1 large **Bramley cooking apple**
25 g (1 oz) **butter**
1 heaped tablespoon **soft brown sugar**
pinch of **ground cinnamon**

step 1 Lightly oil a rectangular baking dish about 10 cm (4 inches) deep – a large pâté dish is ideal. Place overlapping slices of potato around the sides and base of the dish to cover. With a very sharp knife, cut the tenderloin in half and then slice each half lengthways as thinly as possible. Divide the slices into 3 batches and lay a third of the slices over the potato slices in the base. Cover the pork with onion rings and then long, thin strips of carrot. Season well with salt and pepper and sprinkle some of the herbs over the carrot strips. Repeat with 2 further layers of the potato slices, tenderloin slices, onion rings and carrot strips, seasoning after each layer as before. Finish with a final layer of potato slices, which should bring the contents nearly to the top of the dish.

step 2 Mix the Guinness with the stock and mustard in a saucepan and warm gently. Season well with salt and pepper. Bring to a rolling boil and continue to boil until reduced by half and you have a thick, textured sauce.

step 3 Pour the sauce over the pork and vegetables in the baking dish. Cover and bake in a preheated oven, 180°C (350°F), Gas Mark 4, for 45 minutes, then remove the lid and bake for a further 55 minutes until the top is well browned.

step 4 Meanwhile, if making the topping, peel, core and slice the apple. Melt the butter in a small frying pan, and when it begins to bubble, slide in the apple slices. Sprinkle with the sugar and cinnamon and cook for about 1 minute on each side until just crisp.

step 5 Serve the pie in hearty slices, topped with a row of the apple slices, if liked.

It's the appetising taste of Guinness
that goes so well with food

step 4 While the chicken is cooking, cut the whole lime into quarters. Add the lime quarters to the pan about 25–30 minutes through the cooking time.

step 5 Serve each chicken quarter with the pan juices, two lime wedges, the reserved star anise and a watercress salad, if liked.

Lamb with prune, Guinness and walnut stuffing

A touch of the Irish in this classic Moroccan dish permeates the lamb as it gently roasts to create a masterpiece of fusion food.

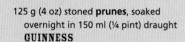

Preparation time 20 minutes, plus soaking
Cooking time 2 hours
Serves 6–8

125 g (4 oz) stoned **prunes**, soaked
   overnight in 150 ml (¼ pint) draught
   GUINNESS
150 g (5 oz) cooked **basmati rice**
50 g (2 oz) **walnuts**, crumbled
1 **garlic clove**, finely chopped
¼ teaspoon **ground cinnamon**
¼ teaspoon **ground cumin**
¼ teaspoon **ground ginger**
¼ teaspoon **ground coriander**
pinch of **ground cloves**
1 **boned shoulder** of **lamb**, about
   1.5 kg (3 lb)
salt and **pepper**

step 1 First make the stuffing. Drain and roughly chop the prunes. Put the prunes in a bowl, add the rice, walnuts and garlic and mix together. Mix the ground spices together, then add to the bowl and mix well.

step 2 Lay the shoulder of lamb out flat and season with salt and pepper. Spread the stuffing over the meat, roll it up and tie securely with clean string.

step 3 Wrap the joint in foil, place in a roasting tin and roast in a preheated oven, 150°C (300°F), Gas Mark 2, for 1½ hours. Remove from the oven, open up the foil and roast for a further 30 minutes until the skin is golden and crisp.

step 4 Leave the lamb to rest for 10 minutes before serving it in thick, juicy slices.

Beef and Guinness puff pastry pie

There is something magical about beef with Guinness, and when it is served in a frame of delicious crisp puff pastry, the combination is irresistible.

Preparation time 15 minutes, plus chilling
Cooking time 1¾ hours
Serves 4

625 g (1¼ lb) **chuck steak**, cut into 2.5 cm (1 inch) cubes
3 tablespoons **plain flour**, seasoned with **salt** and **pepper**, plus extra unseasoned flour for dusting
40 g (1½ oz) **lard**
1 **garlic clove**, finely chopped
5 **shallots**, halved and quartered
400 ml (14 fl oz) draught **Guinness**
1 teaspoon **beef extract**
2 **bay leaves**
leaves from 1 **thyme sprig**
150 g (5 oz) **button mushrooms**
125 g (4 oz) **dried figs**, any stalks removed and quartered
500 g (1 lb) **puff pastry**, thawed if frozen
1 **free-range egg**, beaten, for glazing
chopped **parsley**, to garnish

GUINNESS TIME

How doth the goodly Guinness glass
Improve each dining hour!

How cheerfully it seems to grin,
How creamily it flows!

How does that ruby gleam get in?
Ah, Guinness only knows!

With acknowledgements to Kenn Watts and Lewis Carroll

step 1 Toss the beef with the seasoned flour in a bowl to coat, then shake off any excess flour. Melt the lard in a heavy-based saucepan, add the beef, in batches, and cook until browned all over. Return all the beef to the pan, add the garlic and shallots and cook, stirring, for 3 minutes. Pour in the Guinness and add the beef extract, bay leaves and thyme, scraping all the sediment from the base of the pan. Cover and cook gently for 15 minutes. Add the mushrooms, re-cover and cook for 1 hour until the meat is meltingly tender. Add the figs and cook, uncovered, for 10 minutes until plumped up.

step 2 Meanwhile, roll out the pastry on a lightly floured work surface to a thickness of about 5 mm (¼ inch). Cut 4 x 15 cm (6 inch) squares from the pastry. On each pastry square, make a cut through the pastry 2 cm (¾ inch) in from the edges to form an inner square, but leaving the inner square in place. Carefully transfer the pastry squares to a baking sheet lined with baking parchment and brush the tops with the egg to glaze. Chill in the refrigerator for 10 minutes.

step 3 Bake the pastry squares in a preheated oven, 200°C (400°F), Gas Mark 6, for 10 minutes until risen and golden. Lift out the inner squares and set aside. Place an outer pastry frame in the centre of each warmed serving plate and fill the cavity with the hot beef mixture. Pop an inner pastry square on top of each inner square of filling to form a lid and serve garnished with chopped parsley.

Steak & Guinness burgers with rosemary & garlic butter

Minced beef is marinated overnight in Guinness, then mixed with roasted red onions, griddled and served topped with rosemary and garlic butter to make a memorable burger.

Preparation time 20 minutes, plus marinating, chilling & freezing
Cooking time 10 minutes
Makes 6 burgers

500 g (1 lb) top-quality **lean minced beef**, ideally from grass-fed Irish beef
150 ml (¼ pint) draught **GUINNESS**
1 large **red onion**, finely diced
olive oil, for drizzling and oiling
3 **smoked streaky bacon rashers**, finely diced
1 teaspoon **creamed horseradish**
1 **free-range egg**, beaten
½ teaspoon **paprika**
2 heaped tablespoons **plain flour**
1 **rosemary sprig**
75 g (3 oz) **butter**, softened
1 **garlic clove**, finely chopped
salt and **pepper**

step 1 Lay the minced beef out in a shallow dish and cover with the Guinness. Using your hands, massage the Guinness into the meat, cover with clingfilm and leave to marinate in the bottom of the refrigerator for at least 12 hours.

step 2 When ready to make the burgers, spread the onion out in a baking dish, sprinkle lightly with salt and drizzle with oil. Scatter the bacon on top. Roast in a preheated oven, 150°C (300°F), Gas Mark 2, for 15 minutes. Leave to cool.

step 3 Lift the beef out of its marinade, gently squeeze out any excess liquid and put the beef in a large bowl. Add the roasted onion and bacon, the horseradish, egg and paprika, season with pepper and sprinkle the flour over. Using your hands, mix together well. Divide the mixture into 6 equal portions and form into round patties about 2.5 cm (1 inch) thick. Carefully lay the patties on a baking sheet lined with greaseproof paper, cover with a second sheet of greaseproof paper and chill in the refrigerator for at least 1 hour and up to 6 hours to firm up.

step 4 Meanwhile, pluck the rosemary leaves from the stem and plunge into boiling water for 30 seconds. Drain, then chop as finely as possible. Add to the softened butter and garlic in a small bowl and beat together well. Lay a piece of clingfilm on a flat surface, form the butter into a sausage about 3.5 cm (1½ inches) in diameter and roll up in the clingfilm. Freeze for 20 minutes until set.

step 5 Lightly oil a griddle pan. Heat until just beginning to smoke, add the burgers and cook over a high heat for about 5 minutes on each side, or until well browned on the outside and just pink inside. Serve immediately, each burger topped with a slice of the rosemary and garlic butter.

Beef cobbler

Long, slow-cooked beef and vegetables, richly flavoured with Guinness and topped with cobblestone scones, make a meal in a casserole that you'll be proud to present at the table.

Preparation time 15 minutes, plus resting
Cooking time 2¾ hours
Serves 4–6

2 tablespoons **vegetable oil**
1 **onion**, roughly chopped
125 g (4 oz) **smoked streaky bacon rashers**, diced
1 **garlic clove**, finely diced
1 small **turnip**, diced
1 **carrot**, diced
2 **celery sticks**, diced
625 g (1¼ lb) **braising steak**, cut into 2.5 cm (1 inch) cubes
1 tablespoon **plain flour**, seasoned with **salt** and **pepper** and mixed with 1 teaspoon **dried mixed herbs**
440 ml (¾ pint) can of GUINNESS
1 tablespoon **clear honey**
1 **bay leaf**
1 tablespoon **Worcestershire sauce**
salt and **pepper**
buttered **kale** or **Savoy cabbage**, to serve

Scones
225 g (7½ oz) **self-raising flour**, plus extra for dusting
½ teaspoon **salt**
½ teaspoon **English mustard powder**
50 g (2 oz) **butter**, diced, plus extra for greasing
125 ml (4 fl oz) **milk**, plus extra for glazing
25 g (1 oz) **Parmesan cheese**, freshly grated

step 1 Heat a little of the oil in a large frying pan, add the onion and bacon and cook gently for 5 minutes. Add the garlic and cook, stirring, for 2 minutes. Using a slotted spoon, transfer the onion, bacon and garlic to a casserole, retaining the juices in the pan. Add the turnip, carrot and celery to the pan and cook for 5 minutes, then transfer with a slotted spoon to the casserole.

step 2 Toss the beef with the seasoned flour in a bowl, then shake off any excess flour. Add the beef to the frying pan, in batches, and cook until lightly browned all over, adding the remaining oil as required.

step 3 Transfer the beef to the casserole. Stir the Guinness into the frying pan, scraping all the sediment from the base of the pan. Add the honey, bay leaf and Worcestershire sauce, then pour the contents of the pan into the casserole. Season with plenty of pepper, cover and cook in a preheated oven, 150°C (300°F), Gas Mark 2, for 2 hours.

step 4 Meanwhile, make the scones. Sift the flour, salt and mustard together into a bowl. Add the butter and rub in with your fingertips until you have fine breadcrumbs. Add the milk to a well in the centre of the flour and gradually mix in to form a dough. Knead on a lightly floured work surface until smooth, then roll out to 1.5 cm (¾ inch) thick. Using a 5 cm (2 inch) biscuit cutter, cut out rounds and place spaced out on a lightly greased baking sheet. Leave to rest for 15 minutes.

step 5 Remove the casserole from the oven and check the seasoning. Increase the oven temperature to 200°C (400°F), Gas Mark 6. Brush the scones with milk, scatter with the Parmesan and arrange on top of the casserole, like cobblestones. Return the casserole to the oven and bake for 20 minutes until the scones are golden. Serve with buttered kale or Savoy cabbage.

Haddock in crispy batter with sweet potato chips

Introducing beer to your batter adds magical bubbles to make it extra crispy and light. Adding Guinness creates an exceptional flavour as well.

Preparation time 10 minutes
Cooking time 20 minutes
Serves 2

1 large **sweet potato**
15 g (½ oz) **butter**
125 g (4 oz) **self-raising flour**, plus extra
    for dusting
finely pared **zest** of ½ **lemon**
150 ml (¼ pint) ice-cold draught
    GUINNESS
2 **haddock fillets**, about 175 g (6 oz) each
sunflower oil, for deep-frying
salt and **pepper**

To serve
lemon wedges
parsley sprigs

step 1 Peel the sweet potato and cut into chunky wedges. Melt the butter in a frying pan, add the potato wedges and cook gently for 3–4 minutes. Transfer to a baking sheet, season with salt and pepper and roast in a preheated oven, 180°C (350°F), Gas Mark 4, for about 20 minutes until crisp and golden.

step 2 Meanwhile, sift the flour into a bowl, then add a pinch of salt and the lemon zest. Add the cold Guinness (beer batter must be kept really cold) to a well in the centre of the flour and gradually beat in until the batter is the consistency of thick double cream – don't worry unduly about any lumps.

step 3 Heat enough oil for deep-frying in a deep fryer to 180–190°C (350–375°F), or until a cube of bread browns in 30 seconds. Season the fish fillets with salt and pepper and dust with flour to help the batter stick to the fish. Dip the fillets into the batter to coat, then carefully plunge into the hot oil. Cook for 6–8 minutes, depending on the thickness of the fillets, until the batter is puffed up, crisp and golden. Drain on kitchen paper and serve with the sweet potato chips, lemon wedges and parsley sprigs.

"Now, I feel I've earned a GUINNESS"

Index

Bibliography

Corcoran, Tony *The Goodness of Guinness: The Brewery, Its People and the City of Dublin*, Liberties Press, 2005

Davies, Jim *The Book of Guinness Advertising*, Guinness Publishing Ltd, 1998

Griffiths, Mark *Guinness is Guinness: The Colourful Story of a Black and White Brand*, Cyan Books, 2005

Guinness, Michele *Genius of Guinness: The Enduring Legacy of an Irish Dynasty*, Ambassador-Emerald International, 2005

Hughes, David *A Bottle of Guinness Please: The Colourful History of Guinness*, Phimboy Publishing, 2006

Sibley, Brian *The Book of Guinness Advertising*, Guinness Superlatives Ltd, 1985

Yenne, Bill *Guinness: The 250-year Quest for the Perfect Pint*, John Wiley & Sons, 2007

Acknowledgements

Many thanks to Niamh Carney, Fergal Murray, Justin O'Connor, Eibhlin Roche and Deirdre Flood for all their help, advice and information, and to Fennell Photography for their help in sourcing modern images.

Executive editor Nicola Hill
Senior editor Lisa John
Design Geoff Fennell
Photographer Dan Jones
Home economist Joanna Farrow
Props stylist Rachel Jukes
Senior production controller Amanda Mackie

ACKNOWLEDGEMENTS